Leila Fielding

Female Genocidaires during the Rwandan Genocide

When women kill

Anchor Compact

Fielding, Leila: Female Genocidaires during the Rwandan Genocide: When women kill, Hamburg, Anchor Academic Publishing 2013
Original title of the thesis: Female Génocidaires: What was the Nature and Motivations for Hutu Female Involvement in Genocidal Violence Towards Tutsi Women During the Rwandan Genocide?

Buch-ISBN: 978-3-95489-067-5
PDF-eBook-ISBN: 978-3-95489-567-0
Druck/Herstellung: Anchor Academic Publishing, Hamburg, 2013
Additionally: Manchester Metropolitan University Business School, Manchester, England, Dissertation, 2012

Bibliografische Information der Deutschen Nationalbibliothek:
Die Deutsche Nationalbibliothek verzeichnet diese Publikation in der Deutschen Nationalbibliografie; detaillierte bibliografische Daten sind im Internet über http://dnb.d-nb.de abrufbar

Bibliographical Information of the German National Library:
The German National Library lists this publication in the German National Bibliography. Detailed bibliographic data can be found at: http://dnb.d-nb.de

© Anchor Academic Publishing, ein Imprint der Diplomica® Verlag GmbH
http://www.diplom.de, Hamburg 2013
Printed in Germany

Table of Contents

Abstract

Victimisation of women in times of war, genocide or mass slaughter has been the primary focus of the majority of explorations concerning gender and conflict. Traditionally, women are espoused as victims, at the mercy of male killers and therefore subordinate. The notoriety of brutal, horrific and incomprehensible sexual crimes against women in times of genocide has ensured that reluctance in addressing female accountability has plagued this debate. While examinations of these atrocities are imperative and indispensable in facilitating reconciliation, both psychological and social, this one-sided representation has led to a misunderstanding of the dynamic roles which women play during genocide. Whether supportive, active or auxiliary roles, women have been a vital component in endorsing and sanctioning genocidal violence historically. In Rwanda, some women not only provided assistance and encouragement to Hutu men, but also perpetrated the attacks and incited rape. The suffering of female victims cannot be fully understood without a consideration of the extensive nature of the perpetrators, both male and female. Moreover, quite the opposite of diminishing the value and significance of the victimisation of women, any examination which focuses on female agency re-balances the scales of gender inequality and consequently serves to empower women. Women should not be portrayed solely as victims. Women in the Rwandan genocide were victims and perpetrators, agents and symbols. Gender expectations which propagate the superiority of men both during and after conflict are detrimental to the reconstruction of post-genocide gender identities.

Introduction

This dissertation aims to reveal the largely unexplored dimensions of the roles of women in perpetrating the violence of the Rwandan genocide. What roles did Rwandan women play in the genocide and what were their motives for defying typical established gender norms? Women are presumed to be innately more compassionate than men. Women are cast as guardians of child and home in many cultures and societies. What circumstances drove women to abandon their established gender identity and commit insidious acts against their fellow women? What motives could have destabilised women's affinity to their fellow woman? Does this affinity even exist? Addressing the roles of women as perpetrators of genocide, specifically focusing on the Rwandan case, the aim of the paper is to consider questions concerning the agency of women in genocide. Through an examination of gender and ethnicity, this dissertation hopes to establish that under the correct circumstances and in the right environment, in much larger figures than previously assumed or widely recognised, women can be induced by their own reasoning to be involved in genocidal acts as active agents. Women, when given freedom to do so, are as likely to commit atrocities as are men and do not have to be manipulated by men in order to decide upon this course of action.

This research represents a qualitative, interdisciplinary study based on information provided by news sources, ethnic conflict and genocide literature, feminist literature, reports by non-governmental organisations (particularly the International review of the Red Cross), and international organisations including the United Nations (specifically the International Criminal Tribunal for Rwanda). Primary sources including interviews with convicted killers (especially Jean Hatzfeld's and Nicole Hogg's interviews with perpetrators), printed propaganda (from Tutsi hate newspaper *Kangura*), and oral testimony of female detainees and Rwandan professionals provide the basis for the argument. First, a consideration as to gender theory, gender expectations and feminist theory hopes to reveal a correlation between motivations and gender roles. Second, the paper will evaluate the extensiveness and nature of female involvement. Third, the case study of female genocidaire Pauline Nyiramasuhuko will be investigated. Pauline is a rare case of a female leader during the genocide, yet her story still helps to strengthen the argument that women are sometimes able to assert their own individual agency in times of conflict and when they have the opportunity they can act in much the same manner as men do. Fourth, more broadly, the dissertation will consider the motivations of 'ordinary' women in committing the atrocities to attempt to distinguish whether social, political and circumstantial components were unique to Rwanda, and therefore argue that there were particular features which encouraged unprecedented female participation. Finally, the dissertation will conclude by considering the implications of female involvement in the genocide on post-genocide Rwanda, specifically focusing on gender identity and consequent social and psychological reconciliation.

The dissertation will posit that female genocidaires had a multitude of motivations which cannot be neatly categorised. The nature of female perpetrators involvement was largely guided by gender roles scripted by Rwandan society. Reasons for violence and the forms it took were ideologically motivated. Brutal sexual torture and rape and the women who sanctioned it were a foreseeable consequence of gendered propaganda which dehumanised Tutsi women. Women in leadership roles committed violence and ordinary women contributed in their own specific way to the bloodshed in key auxiliary roles, and, less often in outright murder. The dissertation argues that motivations like fear and gendered propaganda influenced women to commit genocidal offences.

CHAPTER ONE

Gender and Conflict

Conceptions of gender have been fluid and dependant on social circumstances. Gender is an "intersubjective social construction that constantly evolves with changing societal perceptions and intentional manipulation."[1] Ideas of femininity in one nation may wholly contradict what it means to be a woman in another. In times of war and conflict women often have the opportunity to bridge the gender barrier and allowances are made for women to embody stereotypically masculine roles.[2] Still, these supplementary roles which women are allocated during times of conflict are generally in addition to obligations which were widely expected of them pre-conflict. Women are thus required to continue with their responsibilities as carers of the family and home, whilst also functioning in an entirely new capacity. Two of the most common roles for women to perform during the Rwandan genocide were looting and espionage. Most Rwandan women were allowed to be involved in the genocide in subsidiary roles, yet others played more direct roles in the atrocities. To what extent altered gender roles consequently affect gender identities in post-genocide society is in dispute and still under scrutiny. Remarkably, in Rwanda, post-genocide women's roles have gone through a drastic transition. Gender is therefore not a stable construct. Expectations for females differ depending on circumstance, era, age, class, race, nationality and culture, the list could go on. Hence, it is absurd to assume that gender is based upon a biological divide between men and women.

---

[1] L. Sjoberg & C. E. Gentry, *Mothers, Monsters, Whores: Women's Violence in Global Politics* (New York: Palgrave Macmillan, 2007), p. 5.
[2] S. Blizzard, 'Women's Roles in the 1994 Rwanda Genocide and the Empowerment of Women in the Aftermath,' *Georgia Institute of Technology,* http://smartech.gatech.edu/bitstream/handle/1853/11577/blizzard_sarah_m_200608_mast.pdf?sequence=1 (2006), p. 7.

Post-structuralist feminist philosopher Judith Butler has argued that cultural gender and biological sex are a socially constructed phenomenon.[3] Biological sex has formed the foundation on which the construction of gender has been built. In Butler's view, gender norms are reinforced by repetition and encouraged by a social precedent of accepted behaviour. Gender is therefore a rehearsed act or performance scripted by hegemonic social conditions and ideologies, rather than an innate state which is based on one's biological organs. We perform the role expected of us by society. Butler has termed this as 'gender performativity.'[4] In relation to the Rwandan genocide, Butlers views have resonance due to female roles in Rwandan society. Gender performativity in pre-genocide Rwanda could be described as unbalanced, and, for the most part, female gender performances were scripted by a patriarchal culture which endorsed women as second class citizens. Women during the genocide did, for the most part, perform typically 'feminine' coded tasks including encouragement, tactical and operational support and espionage. Yet, a significant number of women perpetrated violence themselves. There could be a few explanations for this. One would propose that women, when given the opportunity to enact power denied them for the majority of their lives, wholeheartedly embraced this chance to assert authority. Another suggests that it was a necessary measure as the ferocity and meticulousness of this particular genocide called for the inclusion of all of Hutu society. The success of the genocide, almost one million people were killed in approximately 100 days, relied on full social conformity. Not only because the murder of each individual victim often required more than one killer, but also as a means to promote shared social and ethnic complicity. In this respect, necessity during the Rwandan genocide sometimes outweighed gender customs.

---

[3] J. Butler, *Gender Trouble: Feminism and the Subversion of Identity* (New York: Routledge, 1990), pp. 135–41.
[4] Ibid.

Any discussion concerning the perpetrators of the Rwandan genocide immediately conjures images of a band of machete wielding, brightly dressed, crazed men roaming and hunting for their Tutsi prey in the popular imagination. Men are automatically presumed to be more intrinsically inclined to commit violence in popular perceptions. Yet, while male members of the Interhamwe, public and militia constituted the majority of the killers, there is the lesser discussed component of female genocide perpetrators to consider. Sarah Blizzard has stated that "there are many shocking aspects of the Rwandan genocide, including the incredible speed with which almost a million people were killed, but perhaps the most appalling reality is that women took part as perpetrators of the most heinous crimes, often against other women."[5] This aspect of female involvement has largely gone unexplored due to precedents which connect agency of violence to men and assume women to be more passive. War and militarisation, for example, are customarily understood as masculine, while civilian and peace-keeper roles are comprehended as feminine.[6] Carol Smart has studied women, crime and criminology from a feminist critique and has asserted that rhetoric concerning crime almost always describes the actor as male. For Smart, it is always *his* rationality, *his* motivation, *his* alienation or *his* victim.[7] However, despite a prevalence of assumptions which cast the criminal, deviant, killer or agent as typically male, women are just as capable of asserting their agency and committing insidious acts. This view is shared by Marie-Chantal, the Hutu wife of a boss during the genocide, and, as she so astutely observes: "a person's wickedness depends on the heart, not the sex."[8] Similarly, a female genocide suspect in Kigali Central Prison has stated that she believes "that women are

---

[5] Blizzard, 'Women's Roles', p. 33.
[6] Blizzard, 'Women's Roles', p. 7.
7 C. Smart, Women, Crime, and Criminology: A Feminist Critique (London: Routledge, 1976), p. 177.
[8] J. Hatzfeld, *A Time for Machetes: The Rwandan Genocide: The Killers Speak* (New York: Farrar, Straus and Giroux, 2005), p. 102.

just as guilty of this genocide as men."[9] In reality, as Jill Steans has noted, it is probably the case that women's peacefulness is as mythical as men's violence.[10]

Eva Fogelman expounds ideas that women traditionally have been socialised to be sympathetic towards the needs of others and tend to respond to them in nurturing ways.[11] Fogelman highlights the contradiction in the assumption that women were more likely to rescue Jews than men and puts this inconsistent view in perspective by asserting that men were just as likely to show compassion as women. Conversely, in his essay investigating the rescuers of Jews during the Holocaust, Philip Friedman hypothesised that women may have been more sensitive than men to the ordeal of the Jews, and especially Jewish children, and may have been more prone to help because they were "more easily moved by their emotions than men,"[12] and thought less of the consequences. Fundamentally though, Friedman's ideas are outdated and based on the assumptions of a patriarchal society. At the end of the twentieth century, popular culture was inundated with an emphasis on the differences between men and women, in particular with their psychological characters. Friedman's perspective may now be perceived as sexist, not least because he assumes that women thought less of the consequences of their actions. Without socially constructed gender norms which have subconsciously guided these studies, perhaps research would have looked for more probing analyses. Friedman concluded exactly what he was psychologically programmed to assume, that women are more empathetic and therefore more likely to intervene or help others. Principally,

---

[9] N. Hogg, 'Women's Participation in the Rwandan Genocide: Mothers or Monsters', *International Review of the Red Cross,* 92, 877 (2010), p. 69.
[10] J. Steans, *Gender and International Relations: An Introduction* (New Jersey: Rutgers University Press, 1998), p. 92.
[11] E. Fogelman, *Conscience and Courage: Rescuers of Jews during the Holocaust* (New York: Anchor Books, 1994), ch. 13.
[12] Philip Friedman, *Roads to Extinction: Essays on the Holocaust* (New York: Jewish Pubn Society, 1980), pp. 411-14.

women are represented and romanticised as "fragile, removed from reality, and in need of protection in a way that the protector receives substantial honour of success."[13] Notions of females as 'beautiful souls,' an idealistic theory formulated by Hegel via Elshtein,[14] ultimately result in portrayals of women as incompetent, or unlikely to commit violent behaviour.[15] Women are subsequently "expected to be against war and violence, but cooperate with wars fought to protect their innocence and virginity."[16] Granting males agency and will in the perpetration of violence, this belief system fails to recognise women as correspondingly competent perpetrators of evil. Although women have not been involved in genocide to the same extent as men, a significant portion of women have wilfully and intentionally engaged in war and genocide.

These assumptions concerning women have been formed by expected gender norms and hegemonic social conditions which have cast women in subordinate roles historically. Women are presumed to be more passive, sensitive and empathetic than men. In armed conflict, mass murder and war, female killers become cast as monstrous, evil, unnatural, deviant and sub-human, while men are protectors, saviours, brave and heroic.[17] Female violence therefore falls outside the boundaries of our received narratives and remains formless.[18] Women who commit atrocities are classified as masculine and lose their femininity. Femininity and violence are conflicting forces. Masculinity and violence are complimentary allies. It is for this reason that female killers are sensationalised in both fiction and reality. In history, women

[13] Sjoberg & Gentry, *Mothers, Monsters*, p. 4.
[14] Ibid.
[15] Sjoberg & Gentry, Mothers, Monsters, p. 165.
[16] Sjoberg & Gentry, *Mothers, Monsters*, p. 4.
[17] A. Jones, *Gender Inclusive: Essays on Violence, Men, and Feminist International Relations* (London: Routledge, 2009), p. 148-149.
[18] J. B. Elshtain, *Thinking about Women and International Violence*, in *Women, Gender, and World Politics: Perspectives, Policies, and Prospects*, edited by P. R. Beckman & F. D.Amico (Westport, CT: Bergin and Garvey, 1994), p. 115.

who do not conform to expected gender roles and embody typically masculine traits are cast as deviant. For example, historical occurrences of women who bridge the gender boundary and either fight in war time or kill are marvelled at, and often create a legacy. Joan of Arc is the archetypal gender transgressor, depicted in popular culture as manly both in appearance and demeanour. Female serial killers, another prime example of how popular culture champions melodramatic depictions of violent women, demonstrate that brutal women are awed at. Interpretations of the story of American serial killer Aileen Wournos, infamously known as 'monster,' have invariably embellished her lesbianism and prostitution. Aileen has been stripped of all typically feminine traits in order to be allowed to be a killer. While these women are a minority, they still demonstrate that women are more than capable of murder, violence and brutality without having been guided by men.

While one would think that instances of female brutality would result in a re-evaluation of gender assumptions, quite the opposite is actually true. Female killers are perceived as the exception, their choices are generally linked to either an inherent, atypical presence of masculine traits or thought to be guided by male manipulation. Masculinity is a recurring motif which dominates any and all portrayals of female mass murderers. In the case of Rwanda, where women conformed to gender traditions and indirectly took part in the genocide by informing on Tutsis or providing support for example, less moral accountability is accredited to them, both by the women themselves and by the courts.[19] Conversely, women who defied gender and cultural stereotypes by choosing to play a more direct role in the genocide have often been labelled evil or non-women. Consequently, these women have been treated

---

[19] Hogg, 'Women's Participation', p. 70.

with the full force of the law in much the same manner as men.[20] Paradoxically, females who perpetrate violence destabilise the very foundations of feminism by stepping outside the gender barrier which has for so long enclosed feminist assumptions. Violent women thus disrupt feminist images of liberated women as capable, equal and not prone to 'male' mistakes or idiosyncrasies such as violence and greed.[21] "Female perpetrators fall outside of traditional discourse on gender roles in war and the Rwanda case reveals that women no longer fit squarely into traditional understandings of females as peace-makers."[22] In many ways gender roles are shaped by war, but also help shape war and the actions taken during conflict.[23]

Comprehensions of modern genocide, particularly the motives and enabling factors which contribute to these instances of mass slaughter, are incomplete without a consideration as to the roles of women as agents, both active and passive, and as enablers. It is vital to note female involvement in the Rwandan genocide in order to challenge patriarchal dominance. Even when women are recognised as having played a role in genocide other than that of victim they are represented as unnatural. Women are denied all agency and rarely permitted the deserving title of perpetrator. Thus, discourse promotes perceptions "wherein women are not allocated free will in their decision to perpetuate and contribute to genocide."[24] Often their actions are justified through insinuations of male manipulation. Frequently, females who kill are alleged to have been already living outside traditional gender boundaries before they committed their crimes. Their already established gender non-conformity subsequently serves as a rationalisation of their actions. These women are gender trans-

---

[20] Hogg, 'Women's Participation', p. 70-71.
[21] Sjoberg & Gentry, *Mothers, Monsters,* p. 1.
[22] Blizzard, 'Women's Roles', p. 6.
[23] Ibid.
[24] H. Gulaid, 'Ordinary Women: Understanding Female Agency in Genocide Perpetration,' *Asbarez* (2011) http://asbarez.com/93363/ordinary-women-understanding-female-agency-in-the-perpetration-of-genocide/ [accessed 2/3/2012]

gressors, and popular understanding of the female perpetrators of the Rwandan genocide has its fair share of insinuations which allude to the killers 'masculine' tendencies. But, if one tried, could one not find at least one stereotypically masculine trait present in almost all of womankind? These contentions are mere fabrications. She killed because she was not a mother, or because she was already brutalised, or because she had been subjected to manipulation by her husband are the proclamations which have now become a feature in Rwandan rhetoric.[25] Yet, these are excuses which conveniently allow for the continuation of categorisations of gender which are both a cultural and social myth. Is it not now time that society recognises the equality of all humankind, and, most importantly, admits that all humans are capable of committing the most heinous barbarisms if placed in the right circumstances? To understand genocide it is imperative that we recognise that women can be, and in the specific case of Rwanda that they *were*, active agents of horrific mass killings and mass rapes.[26] Fundamentally, the perpetual exclusion of women from our comprehension of genocide will invariably generate a distorted image of the psychology of genocide.

In his chapter *Gendering Genocide*, Adam Jones highlights the direct involvement of women in genocide historically.[27] Women have been involved in genocides including The Jewish Holocaust, Cambodia, Armenia, and of course Rwanda.[28] Jones believes that the gender aspect in Rwanda is more multi-faceted than any genocide in history.[29] Highlighting several key points including an historical gender crisis, a gender imbalance of survivors and a pronounced character of gendercidal

---

[25] C. Sperling, 'Mother of Atrocities: Pauline Nyiramasuhuko's Role in the Rwandan Genocide', *Fordham Urban Law Journal*, 33, 2 (2005), p. 116.
[26] Gulaid, 'Ordinary Women,' (2011)
[27] A. Jones, *Genocide: A Comprehensive Introduction* (London: Routledge, 2006), p. 481.
[28] Jones, *Genocide*, ch. 13.
[29] Jones, *Genocide*, p. 481.

reprisals during and after the genocide by the RPF, Jones recognises that although many of these components have been present in other genocides, women's complicity in perpetrating the attacks is truly unique to Rwanda. Jones has identified that the Rwandan Holocaust is exceptional in the annals of genocide for the prominent roles which women played as organizers, instigators and followers.[30] Using African Rights report *Not So Innocent: When Women Become Killers*[31] as the basis for his argument, Adam Jones has provided several profiles of female killers including a councillor, a teacher and an administrator for his article in the *Journal of Genocide Research*.[32] These women all contributed directly to the genocide, councillor Rose Karaushara from Kigali, for example, is accused of ordering the murders of as many as five thousand Tutsis.[33] Jones argues that the Rwandan genocide reveals that the equation of women and peace previously accepted can no longer be authenticated.[34] Due to the unprecedented inclusion of women in these heinous acts, gender assumptions connected to genocide must be altered and extended.[35]

Supporting Jones' claims which challenge the gendered assumptions of women as passive bystanders in genocide, James Waller, in his ground-breaking psychological study *Becoming Evil,* argued that female concentration camp guards during the Holocaust murdered as easily as men and were just as sadistic.[36] Despite the pervasiveness of the earlier explored assumptions pertaining to women's heightened empathy over that of men, Waller notes that female camp guards showed "little

---

[30] Ibid.
[31] African Rights, *Rwanda: Not So Innocent: When Women Become Killers* (London: African Rights, 1995)
[32] A. Jones, 'Gendercide and Genocide', *Journal of Genocide Research*, 2, 2 (2010), pp. 185-211.
[33] A. Jones, 'Gender and Genocide In Rwanda', *Journal of Genocide Research*, 4, 1 (2002), p. 83.
[34] Jones, 'Gender', p. 88.
[35] Jones, 'Gender', p. 89.
[36] J. Waller, *Becoming Evil: How Ordinary People Commit Genocide and Mass Killing* (Oxford: Oxford University Press, 2002), p. 267.

noticeable compassion for 'fellow' women prisoners."[37] Waller uses sources which support his claim including trial records, memoir literature and camp administration literature. Another scholar who propositioned theories concerned with criminal women, Otto Pollak, argued that women commit more crimes than official figures indicate. Pollak claims women's crimes are much more clandestine than men's and that "the lack of social equality between the sexes has led to a cultural distribution of roles which forces women in many cases into the part of instigator rather than performer of an overt act."[38] The majority of feminist criminologists over 60 years after he put forward these theories label Pollak as a misogynist whose ideas are detrimental to feminist scholarship. However, some observers approve of his hypothesis that "the criminality of women is largely masked criminality."[39] It seems that women, when allowed to assert their agency, are just as capable and likely of committing insidious acts as are men.

What is interesting about the Rwandan genocide and the involvement of women is the hands on approach which was a feature of the 1994 slaughter. While female guards and the public during the Holocaust were able to psychologically detach themselves from murder with the gas chambers or simply turning the other way functioning as a psychological barrier, women in Rwanda used machetes and incited rape in a much more extreme approach. The killing tools which each possessed were defined by the culture and technology of the regime. Sharlach has noted that the tools of genocide in Rwanda, mainly machetes, clubs, sticks and other crude

---

[37] Ibid.
[38] Otto Pollak (1950), as cited in Patricia Pearson, *When She Was Bad: Violent Women and the Myth of* Innocence (New York: Viking, 1997), pp. 20–21.
[39] Ibid.

weaponry usually meant that several killers per victim had to be involved.[40] There-fore, for strategic purposes, as well as psychological reasons, it was important to include women. Rwandans did not have the means to distance themselves. Mamda-ni has pointed out that unlike the Nazi Holocaust the Rwandan genocide was not carried out from afar by a small percentage of the population, nor hidden from view, and required full cooperation of the Hutu community, including women, who cheered their men and functioned in vital auxiliary roles.[41] This fact begs the question as to whether Rwandan women were more naturally barbaric or brutal than other female genocidaires in history. Or whether there was something more powerful about the motivating factors which drove them to kill. One argument would assert that women who are denied authority in society, as the majority of Rwandan women were, are more prone to grasp at any power they can appropriate. Another may affirm that there was a profound ideological atmosphere which was bolstered by propaganda which meant women were likely to participate, and this theory will be discussed later in chapter four.

Sjoberg and Gentry do not share Jones' focus on specific cases of female perpe-trators as they believe that these studies are accompanied by gendered suppositions regarding how they came to participate.[42] These scholars assert that sensational accounts of female killers accentuate the peculiarity of particular women as agents.[43] They state that a "skewed gender picture of the genocide in Rwanda" is proposi-tioned by a preoccupation with female perpetrators.[44] They argue that although there was a large involvement of women in comparison to other genocides, the actual

---

[40] L. Sharlach, 'Gender and Genocide in Rwanda: Women as Agents and Objects of Genocide', *Journal of Genocide Research*, 1, 3, (1999), p. 387-388.
[41] M. Mamdani, *When Victims Become Killers: Colonialism, Nativism, and the Genocide in Rwanda* (Oxford: James Currey Ltd, 2001), p. 5.
[42] Sjoberg & Gentry, *Mothers, Monsters*, p. 147.
[43] Ibid.
[44] Sjoberg & Gentry, *Mothers, Monsters*, p. 160.

amount of Rwandan women who took part when contrasted to Rwandan men was minimal. They directly challenge Jones by suggesting that he consistently enforces the prominence of women in leadership roles over the stories of male genocidaires.[45] Feminist ideology has inspired Gentry and Solberg's views that contemporary women are incessantly idolised and objectified as pristine beings incapable of mass murder or genocidal behaviour. Moreover, they contend that convicted female offenders, instead of supplying a representation of female abilities in the enactment of genocide, are deprived of agency, the severity of their actions reduced to pure chance or as a product of male manipulation.[46] Essentially though, these scholars neglect Jones' focus on the victimisation of men.[47] Jones provides a balanced study and attempts to avoid falling into the all too dominant trap of allowing gender expectations, specifically the portrayal of men as agents and women as victims, guide his analyses.

---

[45] Ibid.
[46] Sjoberg & Gentry, *Mothers, Monsters,* p. 160-164.
[47] Jones, *Genocide,* pp. 200-210.

16

CHAPTER TWO

The Nature of Female Involvement

Motivations of the Hutu women who perpetrated violence cannot be understood in separation from Rwanda's pre-genocide gendered social situation. Women's roles in both the wider historical spectrum and the immediate years prior to genocide were primarily subservient. Rwandan women were secondary citizens in society and inferior in status within the family. In this regard Rwandan women were seen as the property of both the men in their family and of their ethnic group as a whole.[48] Pre-genocide Rwanda had a patriarchal culture, demonstrated by the fact that only a small minority of women held positions in governmental institutions.[49] There are a number of popular Rwandan proverbs which allude to women and perfectly encapsulate the temperament of a disparate society based on gender boundaries: 'the hen does not crow with the cocks'; 'in a home where a woman speaks, there is discord'; and 'a woman's only wealth is a man,' are a few examples.[50] Evidence to validate the argument that women were objects in Rwandan society is demonstrated by the fact that some Hutu soldiers raped women and girls of their own ethnic group. Sometimes sexual violence towards Rwandan women, in spite of ethnicity, was perpetrated during the genocide. Hence, Tutsi female victims were not only sub-human because of their ethnic group, but were also objectified as women, and this made them specifically prone to assault. Rwanda was, and still is, religiously dominated by the Roman Catholic Church. Women are socially limited in their control

---

[48] E. Neuffer, *The Key to My Neighbours House: Seeking Justice in Bosnia and Rwanda* (London: Picador, 2002), p. 272.
[49] Hogg, 'Women's Participation,' p. 94.
[50] Hogg, 'Women's Participation,' p. 71-72.

over labour, land, resources, property and surplus of production.[51] These limits are backed up by law and served as an impetus to the dehumanisation which was a necessary step in steering the country towards genocide.

Rwanda had a diverse mix of inter-ethnic relationships. Marital unions between Tutsis and Hutus were not uncommon in the years prior to genocide.[52] Much more common though, were marriages between Tutsi women and Hutu men rather than unions between Hutu women and Tutsi men.[53] Ethnicity was defined on patriarchal lines, meaning that children of Tutsi women and Hutu men were legally classed as Hutu.[54] Even though these offspring were awarded the full benefits of Hutu citizenship they were still perceived by extremists as racially impure.[55] These marriages not only produced children whose ethnicity was dubious in the eyes of the extremists, but also added to the jealousy some Hutu women felt towards Tutsi females. Miscegenation between Hutu men and Tutsi women, more or less accepted up until the onset of genocide, began to be viewed with resentment. Ironically though, many Hutu men, including some extremists, either had Tutsi wives or Tutsi mistresses with whom they had sired children.[56] Some Hutu women were involved in the violence as they believed it was their obligation to do so in order to halt unions of this kind.

Female involvement was not contained merely to ordinary villagers, housewives or the un-educated. Many professional women also took part, including Government ministers and administrators, journalists, medical professionals, aca-

---

[51] S. Meintjes, M. Turshen & A. Pillay, *The Aftermath: Women in Post-Conflict Transformation* (London: Zed Books, 2001), p. 66.
[52] L. L. Green, 'Propaganda and Sexual Violence in the Rwandan Genocide: An Argument for Intersectionality in International Law', *Columbia Human Rights Law Review*, 33 (Summer 2002), pp. 733-776, 733-755.
[53] C. C. Taylor, 'A Gendered Genocide: Tutsi Women and Hutu Extremists in the 1994 Rwanda Genocide,' *PoLAR: Political and Legal Anthropology Review*, 22, 1 (2008) pp. 42-54, p. 42.
[54] Green, 'Propaganda', pp. 733-755.
[55] Taylor, 'A Gendered Genocide', p. 42.
[56] Taylor, 'A Gendered Genocide', p. 43.

demics, nuns, nurses and school teachers.[57] According to Sharlach "female killers included anyone from prostitutes mobilized to kill children, to schoolgirls who killed their classmates."[58] Moral responsibility for many scholars of the genocide lies with the educated women who took advantage of their experience and standing in the community to incite less prosperous women and men to violence.[59] But, attributing moral blame to one division of female society in this way diminishes the responsibility of many ordinary women who sanctioned, took part, or condoned the violence. Through an examination of the motivations which compelled female leaders and ordinary Rwandan women to perpetrate genocide, this dissertation hopes to establish that regardless of class or education, there was a pervasive hatred towards Tutsi women which justified and sanctioned female on female violence in Hutu perceptions.

In 2002 approximately 100,000 Rwandese people were awaiting trial for their participation in the genocide, about 3,000 accused were women.[60] The number of female suspects reveals that what occurred in Rwanda was dissimilar to previous genocides.[61] In March 2010 almost 2000 Rwandan women remained in Rwandan prisons convicted of genocide related offences.[62] Mamdani, quoting Aloysius Inyumba, the RPF minister in charge of women's affairs in 1995, draws attention to not only the women in custody for genocide related crimes, but also emphasises that there was also approximately 800 children ranging from ages seven to seventeen in detention, the older ones of which were charged with genocide, some of which were

---

[57] Hogg, 'Women's Participation', p. 77, see footnotes.
[58] Sharlach, 'Gender and Genocide', p. 392.
[59] Hogg, 'Women's Participation', p. 70.
[60] N. Itano, '3,000 Rwandan Women Await Trials for Genocide' (2002), http://oldsite.womensenews.org/article.cfm/dyn/aid/1152/context/archive [accessed 10/03/2012]
[61] Blizzard, 'Women's Roles', p. 34.
[62] Hogg, 'Women's Participation', p. 70.

female.[63] Nicole Hogg has pointed out that although only less than six per cent of genocide related detainees in Rwandan prisons are women, this number is incongruous to the amount of women actually involved as accomplices in the slaughter.[64] The Rwandan legal system was flooded after the genocide, to the point where local ground level gacaca courts had to be set up. These hearings were conducted in the community, by the community. Consequently, prosecutors have focused on explicitly violent crimes which are easier to prove and more likely to ensure successful prosecution, despite the Gacaca Law stipulating that indirect involvement by those who revealed hiding places or acted as an accomplice to genocide are subject to the same punishment as actual perpetrators.[65] Many women who directed killers to the hiding places of Tutsis, which may in fact be the greatest area of compliancy on the part of women, have escaped justice. The number, while appearing small, is actually huge. In comparison to women's participation in other genocides, female involvement is unprecedented.[66]

During the Rwandan genocide women worked as chief supporters of the violence and as individual agents of murder. Women condemned other women to death and rape. Women looted their fellow women's homes and bodies. Women also, although less commonly, killed other women directly, with a variety of weaponry.[67] Many women who did not kill directly still aided the swift efficiency of the genocide. Succeeding in remaining within the traditional expectations of their gender by performing auxiliary roles, women nevertheless "lent support to the eliminationist Hutu Power agenda by egging on attack groups, informing on concealed victims, and

---

[63] Mamdani, *When Victims Become Killers,* p. 225.

[64] Hogg, 'Women's Participation', p. 70.

[65] Hogg, 'Women's Participation', p. 81.

[66] Jones, *Genocide,* p. 358.

[67] R. Adler, C. Loyle, and J. Globerman, 'A Calamity in the Neighbourhood: Women's Participation in the Rwandan Genocide', *Genocide Studies and Prevention,* 2, 3 (2007), p. 212.

pillaging property from the dead"[68] In addition to these tasks women were also "prominent as spies (especially prostitutes), and pressured younger Tutsi women to accept their designated fate as sex slaves and concubines for Hutu militia members and other men."[69]

As killer Jean-Baptiste has noted, Rwandan custom dictated that women generally did not use the machete, whether it be for farming or killing. During the genocide, most women prepared the family meal as usual in the morning, and then "during the rest of the day they went looting."[70] It was in this vein that some Rwandan women still led a quasi-normal life and remained within traditional gender norms.[71] They would loot dead bodies and homes during the day, and feed their families, often with the spoils of their endeavours, in the evening. If they found some Tutsi women still alive, it was not unusual for them to mock them or finish off the incomplete deed and take to murder. Genocidaire Adalbert has stated that "the women led a more ordinary life. They house-cleaned, they tended to the cooking, they looted the surrounding area... I know one case of a woman who bloodied her hands out there, a too quick-tempered woman who wanted a reputation for herself. Still, if women happened to come upon some Tutsis hidden in an abandoned house, that was different."[72] Women's plundering actions as accomplices sanctioned the murders in the eyes of their husbands. The motivations for these actions will be discussed later in the paper. Looting and pillaging of Tutsi property lent support to the eliminationist Hutu power agenda.[73] Moreover, the pace of killing would have been significantly stifled were it not for the auxiliary roles which women played. If the men had to

---

[68] Adler et al, 'A Calamity', p. 222.
[69] Blizzard, 'Women's Roles', p. 35.
[70] Hatzfeld, A Time For Machetes, p. 101.
[71] 'Ordinary Women,' (2011)
[72] Hatzfeld, A Time For Machetes, p. 102.
[73] Gulaid, 'Ordinary Women,' (2011)

pillage as well as murder, then they would have less time to hunt down Tutsis. This in turn could have resulted in many more escapees. Most women did not explicitly go out to kill, but to reap the rewards of their husbands victims, however, many were drawn into the killings inadvertently when they came across survivors or women in hiding.

In this regard, espionage and revealing the hiding places of Tutsis was the next logical role which women played. Of the women accused of genocide, most have stories which incorporate the rounding up of Tutsis. Emma Mujawamaria was accused of leading Hutu genocidaires to a hospital in order to kill her Tutsi co-workers. Most women accused of genocide are similar to Mujawamaria in that they are young women, often with children, accused of taking part in the mobs which rounded up and murdered Tutsis.[74] Murder and other forms of violence by female perpetrators was often committed against other females and teemed in sexual undertones. Women came under attack as they were the reproducers of their ethnicity. As Nira Yuval-Davis has argued, far from being solely passive victims in the ideologies and policies of the gender system of their society, women, especially older women, were assigned the role of "cultural reproducers of the nation."[75] They retained some form of power in exerting control over other women who may be perceived as deviants.[76] More often than not, and particularly in Rwanda, as this was the main source of power afforded to women, they became totally embroiled in the role of protector of their group, resulting in extreme measures.[77] Violence perpetrated by women was often gender specific. Hutu genocidaires wanted to eliminate the elite Tutsi population and women were particularly involved in shattering the status of

---

[74] Itano 3,000 Rwandan Women (2002), p. 1.
[75] N. Yuval-Davis, *Gender and Nation* (London: Sage, 1997), p. 23.
[76] Ibid.
[77] Ibid.

Tutsi women who, according to Jones, had for so long been revered as Rwanda's sexual elite in Hutu propaganda.[78] Jones proposes that Hutu women displayed "a kind of gendered jubilation at the comeuppance of Tutsi females."[79] Rape and mutilation of Tutsi women, due to depictions of them as sexually superior, was a probable consequence of the genocide.

The rape was as important as the killing.[80] In a 1996 UN report, Special Rapporteur Rene Degni-Segui stated that "rape was the rule and its absence the exception."[81] So horrific were the rapes and sexual torture that many women paid to be killed instead. It is the incomprehensible likelihood of women inspiring such barbarous acts on their fellow women that make the cases of rape so shocking. Rape has been used as a bounty for warriors historically, yet the Rwandan case is much different. Genocide can be defined as the "intent to destroy, in whole or in part, ethnic, racial, national, and religious groups."[82] Rape served as a tool of genocide on many levels. The rapes and mutilations of Tutsi women fall into the category of genocide because there was a calculated decision to destroy their capabilities as reproductive vessels for their ethnic group. The mutilation of body parts which prevented them having children in the future, the diluting of the Tutsi ethnicity by Hutu rapists impregnating Tutsi women, the deliberate infection of HIV and the social stigma attached to rape victims all ensured that the aftereffects go beyond the physical torture of the rape victims themselves and affect the entire Tutsi ethnic

---

[78] Jones, *Gender*, p. 84.
[79] Ibid.
[80] Sjoberg & Gentry, *Mothers, Monsters*, p. 163.
[81] United Nations, *Report on the Situation of Human Rights in Rwanda submitted by Rene Degni-Segui*, Special Rapporteur of the Commission on Human Rights, under paragraph 20 of the resolution S-3/1 of 25 May 1994, E/CN.4/1996/68, January 29, 1996, p. 7, in Binaifer Nowrojee & Dorothy Q. Thomas, *Shattered Lives: Sexual Violence During the Rwandan Genocide and its Aftermath* (New York: Human Rights Watch, 1996) p. 24.
[82] Jones, *Genocide*, p. 46.

group.[83] "Women and girls are violated to denigrate the men of another racial or ethnic group, to attack their perceived purity or the purity of their ethnic group, or used as a warrior's reward."[84] As rape was the rule and its absence the exception an entire generation has been stifled by these heinous acts.

So varied were the actions of women that certain occurrences deserve attention. In Butare a pregnant woman shot at thousands of unarmed Tutsis and, according to one witness, "threw grenades as if she were sowing beans."[85] Teenagers and women surrounded churches, hospitals and other places which Tutsis had flocked to hoping for refuge and wielding machetes and nail studded clubs, functioned as cheerleaders in inciting men to violence. These women and girls also helped to murder the already wounded, entering churches, schools, football stadiums and hospitals to hack women and children to death.[86] Shockingly some women stand accused of murdering or betraying their own husbands and children.[87] Professionals like the nurses at the CHK Hospital in Kigali and at Butare's University Hospital handed over lists of patients to the Interhamwe and soldiers naming Tutsi colleagues to be killed.[88] Principally, women and girls stole the possessions of the dead and wounded. In agreement with James Waller's thesis concerning the absence of any remorse of concentration camp guards during the Holocaust, there is no apparent evidence which would suggest that women were more willing to show compassion towards Tutsis than men. There are cases of mothers and grandmothers who refused to hide their own Tutsi children and grandchildren; and others still

[83] Sharlach, 'Gender and Genocide', p. 107.
[84] Sperling, 'Mother', pp. 638-649.
[85] Volumes 1-2, *Africa Today*, (1995), p. 51 & p.81.
[86] Gendercide Watch, Case Study: Genocide in Rwanda, (1994)
http://www.gendercide.org/case_rwanda.html [accessed 10/03/2012]
[87] Ibid.
[88] Ibid.

who forced Tutsis taken in by their husbands to leave.[89] In one case, Tutsi women left their children under the protection of Hutu mothers who then turned the children over to the Interahamwe.[90]

Nicole Hogg of the Red Cross has interviewed numerous detainees in Rwandas prisons. In an interview with one genocide suspect, an educated Hutu woman who was married to a Tutsi man, Hogg discovers that most women, according to the prisoner's testimony, did contribute to some degree to the genocide:

> *"I think the majority of women participated in it, but in ways different to men. Their participation was limited to three aspects: First, refusing to hide Tutsis. For the most part, women were not interested in participating in the genocide in a positive sense, but the vast majority did not want to help Tutsis either. Second, assisting the killers; women assisted the killers by preparing the meals, fetching drinks and encouraging their men. Women brought provisions to the roadblocks and fed their men at home. Third, information; women knew a lot. Their eyes were open. In particular, women exposed the hiding places of Tutsis."[91]*

Although this testimony implies that women generally took secondary, auxiliary roles in the genocide, there are also women who already held positions of superiority within the community who used their status to incite, champion and take part in genocidal violence.

---

[89] Ibid.
[90] Sharlach, 'Gender and Genocide', p. 392.
[91] Female genocide suspect, Kigali Central Prison (interview, respondent #13), 3 July 2001, in Nicole Hogg, 'Women's Participation in the Rwandan Genocide: Mothers or Monsters?' *International Review of the Red Cross,* 92, 822 (2010), p. 79. http://www.icrc.org/eng/assets/files/other/irrc-877-hogg.pdf [accessed 20/12/11]

CHAPTER THREE

Women in Leadership Roles

In 2010, forty-seven women were suspected of genocide in 'Category 1.'[92] This classification includes "planners, organizers, instigators and ringleaders of the genocide, as well as those who occupied leadership roles in public administration, political parties, the army and religious denominations, and who committed or encouraged the genocide or crimes against humanity."[93] Some Rwandan Non-Governmental Organisations claim that if women had held more positions of authority in 1994 then the genocide could have been avoided.[94] According to Judithe Kanakuze, co-ordinator of one such organisation, women "have a different nature to men, they are not violent. If there had been more women in power, the genocide would not have taken place."[95] This speculative theory perfectly demonstrates that Rwandan society still remains a society based on gendered assumptions. The fact that some women in leadership roles in 1994 were enthusiastic supporters of the genocide, while others devoted their attention to encouraging others to comply is incompatible with this supposition. Likewise, Venuste Bigirama, of Rwandan NGO ASOFERWA, also agreed and said that: "I really think that if there had been more women in leadership positions, the genocide would not have occurred. Women are more sentimental."[96] These precarious positions which seem to have been favoured

---

[92] Government of Rwanda, Category 1 List, http://www.gov.rw/government/category1.htm (last visited by Hogg 3 September 2009), in Hogg, 'Women's Participation', p. 90.
[93] Article 51 of the Organic Law No. 16/2004 of 19.06.2004 establishing the organisation, competence and functioning of Gacaca courts charged with prosecuting and trying the perpetrators of the Crime of Genocide and other Crimes against Humanity, committed between October 1, 1990 and December 31, 1994 (hereinafter 'Gacaca law'), available at: http://www.amategeko.net/ (last visited by Hogg 11 October 2009), in Hogg, 'Women's Participation', p. 90.
[94] Hogg, 'Women's Participation', p. 90.
[95] Interview with Judithe Kanakuze, National Co-ordinator, Re´seau des Femmes, Kigali, 8 June 2001, in Hogg, 'Women's Participation', p. 90.
[96] Interview with Venuste Bigirama, Technical Advisor, Association for Solidarity between Rwandan Women (ASOFERWA), Kigali, 11 June 2001, in Hogg, 'Women's Participation', p. 90.

by Rwandan NGO's, who most probably have political motives in mind, and are attempting to re-balance the gender inequality which has been a feature of Rwandan institutions for so long, are consistent with the essentialist school of feminist thought. Lisa Sharlach has described this school as theorising that "men are inherently more warlike than are women... Essentialists believe that the wars we have suffered are the result of male-dominated political and military systems. The world would be more peaceful if it were women making policy or reweaving the web of life."[97] The Rwandan genocide, despite these proclamations by NGO's, provides no such evidence to suggest that more women in power could have resulted in a peaceful resolution to the conflict. On the contrary, there were some women who abused their positions for personal motivations and abandoned all sense of obligation to their community.

The case of Pauline Nyiramasuhuko, former Minister of Family and Women's Affairs and member of the elite inner circle of Hutu extremists Akazu (or little house), is an extreme example of a female genocidaire. Her story, while sensational, deserves attention because she is representative of the gender directed violence committed by many other female génocidaires.[98] The choices which she made in how to implement the murders of Tutsi women, namely inciting rape and sexual torture, are indicative of the dehumanisation which had been bestowed upon Tutsis in Rwanda. Described by witnesses as wearing military fatigues and carrying a machine gun as she ordered acts of genocide,[99] Nyiramasuhuko's modus operandi consisted of establishing roadblocks in order to identify, kidnap, rape and kill members of the Tutsi population.[100] Pauline routinely travelled through her native region of Butare in a peugot van during the genocide, driven by her son who was an

---

[97] Sharlach, 'Gender and Genocide', p. 389.
[98] Blizzard, 'Women's Roles', p. 37.
[99] Blizzard, 'Women's Roles', p. 39, also in ICTR, Office of the Prosecutor, Butare Cases: Witness Summaries Grid (6 April 2000), Witness No. 54 (QF), in Hogg, 'Women's Participation', p. 92.
[100] Gulaid, 'Ordinary Women', (2011), also in Hogg, 'Women's Participation', p. 92.

influential member of the Interhamwe, and used a loud speaker to incite the rape and murder of Tutsi women.[101] Compelling motivations are implied by her actions. There must have been a profound hatred towards Tutsi women which motivated her to incite rape on such a massive scale. Her own sister has claimed that Pauline was ardently racist and loathed working with Tutsis at the ministry.[102] Notoriously the first woman to be charged with the perpetration of genocidal rape, Pauline was prosecuted for two counts of rape, one as a crime against humanity and another as a violation of the Geneva Convention on War Crimes.

There is a certain sombre irony to Pauline's case which has made her infamous. Pauline held responsibilities to protect and empower women, yet she chose to callously order the rape, torture and mass murders of her female Rwandan neighbours. Pauline was part Tutsi, yet she provoked crimes against her fellow ethnicity. As a leader Pauline had the opportunity to order the fast execution of victims, yet she chose to prolong the suffering and humiliation of Tutsi women by inciting those under her authority to commit brutal acts of rape and torture. As for motivations of her actions, ICTR investigator Maxwell Nkole has put forward that Pauline Nyiramasuhuko was "convinced by the propaganda, especially the propaganda that caused divisions between women. The myth of the beautiful, arrogant Tutsi woman led to jealousy by Hutu women and an inferiority complex among Hutu women. This seems to have come through in the way she treated Tutsi women."[103] Considering the earlier discussed assumptions pertaining to women's supposed empathy and compassion, does Pauline's story suggest that she was an exception, that her actions are an indication that she possessed masculine traits? Or, does her story

---

[101] Sperling, 'Mother', p. 649.
[102] Blizzard, 'Wonen's Roles', p. 38.
[103] Interview with Maxwell Nkole, ICTR Investigator, Kigali, 11 July 2001, in Hogg, 'Women's Participation', p. 92.

display that women are perhaps not as inclined to demonstrate sympathy as previously assumed, especially when intense jealousy is a component, therefore propositioning that these gendered assumptions are erroneously based on a socially constructed perception of gender? Pauline is not an anomaly as a female perpetrator of mass violence, or as a leader of genocidal atrocities.[104] Catholic nuns, women in the military and the influential Akazu circle which included President Habyarimana's widow Agathe Kanziga have also been accused of Category 1 offences. Furthermore, as previously addressed in chapter two, many more 'ordinary' women were responsible for perpetrating genocidal violence in Rwanda. Pauline's story is now controversial in scholarship of the Rwandan genocide. Sjoberg and Gentry, for example, believe that Pauline has been made an example of and that focus on her role has been detrimental to comprehensions of genocide perpetrators.[105] But, should attention be afforded to her story even though she is a rare example of a female leader? Essentially, it is vital to note her key role in the genocide because to neglect recognition of her participation would ultimately result in a distorted image of female involvement. Yet, at the same time, to over emphasise Pauline's role detracts agency from ordinary women, and, indeed, men.

Carrie Sperling has stated that Pauline's case reveals more about our continued defiance in viewing women as equals than it does about her uniqueness among her female peers and subsequently challenges the myth that women are not capable of being warriors as their roles as mothers and wives prohibits their involvement in depraved acts of violence.[106] The fact that Pauline's case is so scandalous (scholars

---

[104] Sperling, 'Mother', p. 638.
[105] Sjoberg et al, *Mothers Monsters*, p. 4.
[106] Sperling, 'Mother, p. 638.

and journalists have described her as 'monstrous,'[107] evil and a non-woman[108]) establishes a continued defiance in permitting women the deserving title of perpetrator. Pauline's central role as a female genocidaire was an exception. The majority of Hutu women did not incite, nor commit, genocidal or sexual violence on such a massive scale. Most women though, did not possess the freedom, influence or opportunity of leadership which Pauline did. Most women were restricted by gender boundaries and often programmed to perform the gendered roles (such as looting) which Rwandan society had scripted for them. Who is to say how many more women would have become instrumental in the genocidal campaign should Rwandan customs have been more permitting. Of course, this is speculation and conjecture which is based upon a complex fusion of situational suppositions. For example, Pauline's feelings of hate towards Tutsi women were not uncommon, they were shared by many other Hutu women. Interviews with perpetrators corroborate this claim.[109] To view Pauline's acts as incomprehensible because of her gender is to disregard history and contribute to the stereotypical reasoning which disseminates the victimisation of women. Heinous violence is inflicted on women during conflict due to their otherness and their disparity from the patriarchy which propagates conflict. Pauline's case challenges the myth that there is something categorically unique about the female nature which makes women incapable or unlikely to be warriors. Female leaders who committed atrocities during the genocide were social deviants by refusing to conform to gender expectations, but in no respect are they 'monsters.' They actually demonstrate that women, just like men, are capable of great good as well as great wrong. These women had not drifted from their charac-

---

[107] P. Landesman, 'A Woman's Work', in NY Times Magazine, 15 September 2002, available at: http://www.nytimes.com/2002/09/15/magazine/a-woman-s-work.html [accessed 11/01/2012]
[108] Interview with Judithe Kanakuze, National Co-ordinator, Re´seau des Femmes, Kigali, 8 June 2001, in Hogg, 'Women's Participation,' p. 100.
[109] See Hogg, 'Women's Participation', various interviews throughout article.

teristically good selves. Rather, they were convinced by genocidal ideology and motivated by hate and jealousy. Cases like Nyiramasuhuko's present a challenge to established gender identities. "We cannot insist on the strength and competence of women in all the traditional masculine arenas," states social scientist Pearson, "yet continue to exonerate ourselves from the consequences of power by arguing that, where the course of it runs more darkly, we are actually powerless. This has become an awkward paradox in feminist argument."[110] Female leaders such as Pauline Nyiramasuhuko, largely due to the status of Rwandan women in pre-genocide society were rare, yet the role she played reveals that the expectation that women are intrinsically inclined to make peace rather than war can no longer be upheld.[111]

---

[110] P. Pearson, *When She Was Bad: Violent Women and the Myth of Innocence*, (New York: Viking, 1997), p. 32.
[111] Blizzard, 'Women's Roles', p. 42-43.

CHAPTER FOUR

Motivations of 'Ordinary' Women

The term 'ordinary' women encompasses those who were not leaders, those who did not hold prominent roles within the Rwandan media and those who could not be classed as a ringleader during the genocide. These women were generally accused of category two or three offences which correspondingly relate to those who perpetrated the genocide and their collaborators and those who looted the dead and barely living and their homes.[112] Trials for category two and three offences have been conducted by the gacaca tribunals since 2004. This unique trail system imposes a maximum sentence for category two perpetrators as life imprisonment. Classification of suspects thus plays a crucial role in determining the subsequent stage for trial and the sentence involved.

The reasons for women's participation in the Rwandan genocide are as varied as the nature of their involvement.[113] Every woman's choices were motivated by a convergence of factors which were unique to an individual's particular circumstances. Nevertheless, research conducted by scholars who have interviewed female perpetrators indicate three main common themes, as well as three subsidiary causes which complimented each other and created the atmosphere which was necessary for the erosion of moral barriers to occur. These motivations overwhelmed any kinship which women felt towards each other and made violence possible, and in some cases, a probable outcome. The accused have cited fear and coercion, which was strengthened by a deeply ingrained habit in Rwanda of obeying orders from authority, an intense anti-Tutsi propaganda which endorsed jealousy and envy, and

---

[112] Hogg, 'Women's Participation', p. 76.
[113] Hogg, 'Women's Participation', p. 83.

complimented ideological rationale which overrode any sense of gender affinity between women. The varied nature of these factors demonstrates that women's motivations cannot be neatly categorised and were the result of highly complex conditions. These motivations help to explain why ordinary Rwandan women chose to perpetrate, or induce, brutal attacks against their female Hutu neighbours.

Before the genocide women are shown to have been second class citizens. This uneven power structure must be taken into account when thinking about intimidation and pressure tactics. Not to lose sight of the varied social relationships is, however, paramount. While some Hutu women lived by established gender boundaries, others had become socially, and culturally, mobile. Some women, already known for pushing social boundaries before the genocide, found their non-conformist personalities made participation possible. One witness has pointed out that "there were some bad-mannered girls whose friends were Interahamwe. They must have walked together with their Interahamwe boyfriends and thus saw their deeds. When you keep on exchanging ideas with someone, you may find room within yourself to accommodate those ideas."[114] With this said, these women were rare, the majority of women were restricted by Rwandan gender expectations and subordinate to their husbands. Socially, women were a scarcity in the public services and political arenas and remained largely in the home. Even with the secondary status of Rwandan women considered, genocidal actions inspired by fear justifiably endures as a controversial topic amongst historians. Without having lived in a time of oppression, without having experienced an omnipresent fear, judgement must be reserved on the part of the retrospective spectator.

---

[114] Adler et al, 'A Calamity', p. 213.

33

In numerous interviews female prisoners have frequently specified that fear had a role in persuading them to participate in the genocide. Sometimes, women were not directly threatened, but even so held considerable fear of the consequences if they refused cooperation.[115] African Rights also reports detailed testimonies of people, including women, who participated in the massacres under threat.[116] These explanations sometimes seemed doubtful. Especially when other women in detention who were interviewed said they were able to continue defending people in their homes by bribing the Interahamwe to look the other way. "In other cases," points out Hogg, "the explanations provided were highly credible, especially where women did not have the security of menfolk in their household.[117] Women often participated in the violence by revealing Tutsis to the Interhamwe or bargaining one Tutsi life in order to save another. Yet, at the same time as assisting the killers some women also assisted the hunted.[118] It is this paradox which ensures that female actions cannot be neatly catalogued as being driven exclusively by fear. In one case, a woman testified that she chose to bargain the life of an older Tutsi woman after being threatened by one of the Interhamwe. She was already protecting two Tutsi girls in her home and made a conscious choice to save the lives of the two younger girls in exchange for the life of an "old woman, who was already sick and might not have survived anyway."[119] Following this event the woman became friends with some members of the Interhamwe who continued to look the other way. In addressing the effect of fear the witness stated that: "Although I was a bit scared of them, they also feared me because I had a gun. (I got the gun when people threatened to

---

[115] Hogg, 'Women's Participation', p. 84.
[116] African Rights, *Rwanda: Death, Despair and Defiance* (African Rights, London, 1995) pp. 995–1000.
[117] Hogg, 'Women's Participation', p. 84.
[118] Hogg, 'Women's Participation', p. 86.
[119] Hogg, 'Women's Participation', p. 85-86.

kill my aunt. I told them if they hurt her I would kill them, or have them killed by Habyarimana's cousins, who were friends of mine.)"[120] Although fear of reprisals by the Interhamwe guided some decisions in assisting the killers, some women were also able to bribe, challenge, manipulate or bargain for the lives of Tutsis. There was no set directive when it came to what allowances should be deemed acceptable. This was a genocide conducted by friends, neighbours, in some cases relatives, and therefore there were routes of negotiation.

Sceptics of the testimony of prisoner's who emphasise the role of fear would suggest that their focus on fear and coercion conveniently functions as a means to attempt to avoid or lessen punishment, especially when viewed in the context of pre-trial testimonials. Gender expectations which stipulated that women should comply with their husband's orders provide a credible explanation as to why women unquestionably supported the genocide. But, the reasons for the involvement of women are much more multifaceted than this explanation would propose. The majority of Hutu women, due to ideological beliefs, wanted to take part in the slaughter. Tutsis were viewed and dehumanised as cockroaches, a superior minority who deserved to be stripped of their arrogance by humiliation. When female detainees indicate fear as a motive, blame shifts to society rather than the individual. Any focus on actions taken by women due to fear ultimately bolsters male superiority by way of playing into the stereotype of women as weak and easily led. But is Rwandan society distinctly defined by an undertone of male manipulation? Or do women have some power in manipulating their husbands?

Psychological motivations which inspire confessions of this nature must also be taken into account. Guilt and conscience can be alleviated by way of convincing

---

[120] Ibid.

oneself that there was no personal agency involved, no choice was available. Certainly though, choices are made in times of genocide. Mark Drumbl, doubts that coercion was a major factor, even among male genocide participants.[121] Conversely, in their study *Shattered Lives*, Human Rights authors have stated that "ordinary citizens acted from fear, both fear of the Tutsi whom they had been taught were coming to kill them, and fear of other Hutu who threatened reprisals on any who did not join in the carnage."[122]

Interestingly, when a study which interviewed a cross section of ten female perpetrators attempted to uncover why rank and file Rwandan women assaulted or murdered targeted victims during the genocide was conducted by Adler, Loyle, and Globerman, they found that some women said they feared they would be considered Tutsi sympathisers if they did not take part. This fear was not wholly irrational, moderate Hutus were also the targets of attacks.[123] One woman spoke of how her husband tried to sensitise her to Hutu power ideology, and how he insisted participation was obligatory.[124] "Personally," she said, "I never was on their side, but my husband once said to me, 'If you don't take part, I will kill you myself.' So I agreed to participate"[125] Of course, these women were accused of genocide, and so their testimony cannot automatically be taken at face value.

Overwhelmingly, Hutu women would reveal the hiding places of Tutsi women and children. Nicole Hogg has noted that perhaps this is the largest area of compli-

---

[121] M. A. Drumbl, 'Punishment, Post genocide: From Guilt to Shame to Civis in Rwanda', in *New York University Law Review*, Vol. 75, No. 5, November 2000, pp. 1247–48.
[122] B. Nowrojee & D. Q. Thomas, *Shattered Lives: Sexual Violence During the Rwandan Genocide and its Aftermath* (New York: Human Rights Watch, 1996) p. 14.
[123] H. Gulaid, 'Ordinary Women: Understanding Female Agency in the Perpetration of Genocide,' *The Armenian Weekly* (2011) http://www.armenianweekly.com/2011/01/21/ordinary-women-understanding-female-agency-in-the-perpetration-of-genocide/ [accessed 02/03/2012]
[124] Gulaid, 'Ordinary Women' (2011)
[125] Adler et al, 'A Calamity', p. 216.

ance on the part of Hutu women.[126] These instances do not seem congruous with the assertion that fear was a major factor. Hutu women could have opted to profess ignorance as to the whereabouts of Tutsis in hiding. Moreover, while it is doubtful that women could have stopped the genocide as some NGO's spokeswomen have suggested, wives could have encouraged their husbands to kill without torturing or raping their female victims, or to lessen the pace, or to show compassion. Some women convinced their husbands to let Tutsis hide in their houses. It was a complex predicament; some men would go out and kill during the day while hiding friends and relatives, demonstrating brutality and compassion bilaterally. Moral outcry could have had an effect on continuation of the genocide. Rwandan women were the moral heart of the family. According to a female genocide suspect interviewed by Hogg "no women criticised their men for being killers. This was not because they feared their husbands but because they believed in the need to kill Tutsis. Imagine the influence women could have had if they had tried to advise their husbands!"[127] Even though many women were taught not to contradict their husbands, there were other meth-ods which could have been taken to express dissatisfaction, if, in fact women were against the violence. Non-verbal communication by way of chastisement in the home could have been one way in which the wives of genocidaires could have attempted to stifle their husband's brutality. As Pancrace, one of the killers studied by Hatzfeld has noted: "my wife did not lecture me, she did not turn away from me in bed. She reproached me only on those days when I overdid it."[128] With this said, fear and coercion remains a controversial issue in genocide scholarship. It is impossible to tell what effect fear can have on human behaviour or to accurately presume how any one person will react to it. Culpability is difficult to ascertain when coercion becomes

---

[126] Hogg, 'Women's Participation', p.78.
[127] Hogg, 'Women's Participation', p. 79.
[128] Hatzfeld, *A Time For Machetes,* p. 100.

a factor. Should a person be forced to kill under duress, does this automatically lessen their moral responsibility? Ultimately, the answer is not a simple one. What must be noted though, is that choices are never fully taken away. The victimisation of the perpetrators should never overshadow the persecution of the victims.

The role of fear should not be overstated. Pre-genocide Rwanda was not a totalitarian state. While there were women who were threatened with violent consequences if they did not obey, women who were forced to reveal the hiding places of Tutsis to save their own families and women who felt so oppressed by their husbands that they dared not intervene, there were also women who willingly led the violence and exploited positions of superiority, women who made no attempt to stop or lessen the killings, women who were active in murder, looting and espionage, and women who took pleasure in humiliating Tutsi women. Heinous sexual crimes committed by men were sometimes cheered on by ordinary Hutu women. Pauline provides an exemplary case in how women incorporated sexual atrocities in the method of murder. Some female perpetrators who cite fear as a motive could be accused of playing up to typical female gender expectations such as blind obedience, weakness or subservience. Yet, what about the traditional Rwandan custom which advocates women as the ethical centre of the family? Sometimes, there was room for manoeuvre on the part of women to influence their spouses actions, particularly considering their influential position on ethical issues within the home. To presume, due to a social precedent of males possessing the authority in the family that every women who took part was coerced, manipulated, feared reprisals or was under orders from her husband is a profound generalisation. One of the aims of the dissertation is to challenge assumptions which remove all agency from female decisions, therefore, it is no surprise that fear and coercion, while undoubtedly a motive for some repressed Rwandan women, cannot be cited as the most significant factor. Men were also subjected to fear and coercion, in an altogether dissimilar, yet on a much more intense scale than women. Thus, fear and coercion cannot be identified as a motivation which should solely be connected to female perpetration of the Rwandan genocide.

Somewhat interlinked with the motive of fear of retribution if one did not comply with male demands is what some have described as a deeply ingrained habit in Rwanda to obey orders from those in authority. Obeying orders from persons in authority is an ingrained habit in almost all nations and is most definitely not a typically unique Rwandan feature. Conformity underpins many professions, especially those connected with war, such as the military, police force and government. Women, on the whole, were used to obeying their husbands and other males in the community. Yet, this does not mean that they lacked other paths of persuasion. Rwandan women were expected to support their husband's decisions on the one hand, while on the other they were urged to influence the actions of men and ensure that they make moral and ethical choices. For centuries women have been gendered as possessing the ability to bend their husbands ear, convince them of the right path to take, or give advice where needed. Even the Hutu Ten Commandments (addressed in the next section) corroborates this claim. In the third commandment, the transcript urges women to bring their men back to sense and away from the Tutsi female seductresses.[129] It is this inconsistency in gendered assumptions which demands a re-evaluation of gender 'norms' and which also reveals a contradiction in the assertion that Rwandan women took part in the violence as they were told to do so. If the women did not believe that violence was a necessary step then presumably

---

[129] Appendix

there would have been more recorded instances of dissent or moral outcry. Females are just as well known for their ability to manipulate men as vice versa. To presume that women feared men and obeyed them unquestioningly is to contribute to gendered expectations of men as strong authoritarians and women as weak followers. In some cases it was not men, but other women, who incited violence and championed murder, thus fear of men cannot explain all cases of female participation.[130] One woman in detention pronounced another accused female as "the ringleader of the group. She had so much power. She even used to fight with men. She was very enthusiastic and strong. She didn't have a husband, and didn't even want to take one because she was so strong."[131] The effects of official orders from leaders and the Rwandan government however is a different matter entirely. Many women trusted the countries leaders and believed wholeheartedly that they were in a kill or be killed situation. "The leaders told us that the Tutsis had prepared graves to put the Hutus in and that we had to kill the Tutsis first before they killed us," states one female prisoner, "we believed them because they were educated people. I believed them, and that is why I killed that woman."[132] Official orders and directives were disseminated in virulent hate speeches which dehumanised Tutsis in radio broadcasts and print media steadily throughout the course of the genocide.

Gendered propaganda was a critical component in motivating women who participated in genocide. In the months leading up to the genocide violent sexual imagery of Tutsi females proliferated in the iconography of Hutu extremist literature.[133] Rwandan society was bombarded with radio broadcasts advocating murder

---

[130] Hogg, 'Women's Participation,' p. 86.
[131] Woman convicted of genocide, Gitarama Prison (interview, respondent #10), 2 July 2001, in Hogg, 'Women's Participation,' p. 86 (footnotes)
[132] Woman convicted of genocide, Gitarama prison (interview, respondent #10), 17 July 2001, in Hogg, 'Women's Participation,' p. 87.
[133] Taylor, 'A Gendered Genocide,' p. 42.

and hate speeches condemning Tutsis to death. Radios were even distributed to those who did not possess one so that the message could infiltrate poorer areas of Rwanda as well as the cities. The public were inundated with hate media and propaganda in newspapers and magazines and consistently reminded of their duty to cleanse the nation of the Tutsi 'cockroach' problem. Leaders like Pauline Nyiramasuhuko, Hutu extremist government organisation the Akazu (little house), of which Pauline was a part, and influential members of the Interhamwe enforced these messages and goaded the public into action. Llezlie L. Green has described gender hate propaganda as "perhaps the most virulent component of the propaganda campaign."[134] Lisa Sharlach has pointed out that gendered propaganda sexualised and demeaned Tutsi women in order to set the stage for genocide and mass rape.[135] Nicole Hogg has contended that propaganda also propagated divisions between Rwandan women, by maintaining that Tutsi women were "working for the interest of their Tutsi ethnic group" and likely to appropriate the jobs and husbands of Hutu women.[136]

Propaganda concerning Rwandan women had been a feature for at least four years prior to genocide and had two main facets in Rwandan culture. One branch cast Hutu women in supporting roles during the genocidal campaign, accentuating their duty as guardians of child and home, thus encouraging their involvement in genocidal measures as a defensive precaution to ensure the continuation of their ethnic group.[137] Another, depicting Tutsi women as seductresses who were also enemies of the state, paved the way for sexual atrocities by providing justification

---

[134] Green, 'Propaganda', pp. 733-776, 733-755.
[135] Sharlach, 'Gender and Genocide,' p. 393-394.
[136] Hogg, 'Women's Participation,' p. 87.
[137] Jones, Genocide, p. 488.

reinforced by media endorsed racism.[138] Both forms of propaganda complimented each other. On the one hand, Hutu women were cast in auxiliary positions, their obligations to their menfolk were intensified. While on the other, Tutsi women were cast as enemies of the Hutu race, their sexuality and deviance exaggerated. Drawing on colonial divisions of Tutsi ethnic superiority, Tutsi women were characterised as more beautiful and desirable than Hutu women, yet "inaccessible to Hutu men whom they allegedly looked down upon and were too good for."[139] As addressed in chapter two, pre-genocide Tutsi women were more likely to marry Hutu men than vice versa. Thus, Tutsi women became the crucial antagonists in the Hutu extremists' struggle because "they were socially positioned at the permeable boundary between the two ethnic groups."[140] As a consequence of their precarious position between both ethnicities, Tutsi women's ethnicity and gender made them especially exposed to assault.[141]

Kangura, one of the most influential expressions of hate, was a paper which billed itself as "the voice that seeks to awake and guide the majority people."[142] Its most infamous article, which was first published in December 1990 and reappeared in the paper repeatedly, was titled 'The Hutu Ten Commandments.' Articulating and committing to paper popular preconceptions concerning a doctrine of Hutu purity, the articles first three commandments deal directly with the exclusive beauty of Tutsi women over that of Hutu women and the dangers which are associated with their advanced sexuality. This view, according to journalist Gourevitch, was one which had been persistently fortified by the choices of visiting white men, as well as promi-

---

[138] Jones, *Genocide*, p. 489.
[139] Nowrojee & Thomas, *Shattered Lives,* p. 18.
[140] Taylor, 'A Gendered Genocide', p. 42.
[141] Green, 'Propaganda', pp. 733-776, 733-755.
[142] P. Gourevitch, *We Wish To Inform You That Tomorrow We Will Be Killed With Our Families* (London: Picador, 1999) p. 85.

nent Hutus.[143] Commandment one admonishes men who intermarry, befriend or employ Tutsi women, suggests that Tutsi women's allegiance lies solely with their ethnic group, and casts Hutu men who connect with them as traitors.[144] Consistent with this view, Tutsi women who had relationships with Hutu men were perceived as only using their position to "infiltrate the Hutu ranks."[145] Commandment two focuses on established gender roles of the Hutu woman as mother and wife and puts forward that they are "more suitable and conscientious in their role as woman, wife and mother," than the Tutsi woman.[146] Commandment two thereby strengthens Hutu women's duties to their families and husbands whilst conveniently providing a role which Hutu women can be proud of, over the supposed innately immoral sexual behaviour of the Tutsi woman. This is a powerful ploy considering that Hutu women had largely been stripped of alluring traits and were seeking a role which they could embrace without embodying the implied immoral features of their counterparts. Commandment three stimulates the responsibility of the Hutu woman in providing moral guidance for their husbands, brothers and sons and encourages them to bring them back to reason and away from the Tutsi femme fatales.[147]

Due to propaganda of this nature Tutsi women were cast in a hazardous situation. Hutu women could not be like them, and Hutu men could not have them. This double edged sword served to fuel racial sentiment and paved the way for sexual atrocities committed against Tutsi women. Hutu women, already convinced that they were of lesser sexual value than Tutsis due to a pre-existing social consensus, were inevitably sanctioned to commit crimes by the powerful connotations of these mes-

---

[143] Gourevitch, We Wish, p. 88.
[144] From publisher Hassan Ngeze, 'The Hutu Ten Commandments,' Kangura, issue 6 (December 1990) in S. Totten & R. Ubaldo, We Cannot Forget: Interviews with Survivors of the 1994 Genocide in Rwanda (USA: Rutgers, 2011) p. 199.
[145] A. Thompson, The Media and the Rwanda Genocide (London: Pluto, 2007), p. 365.
[146] Totten, et al, We Cannot Forget, p. 199.
[147] Totten, et al, We Cannot Forget, p. 199.

sages. As sexuality was the focus of much gendered propaganda, it is only natural that forms of violence took a sexual character. Images and characterisations of Tutsi women as sexual objects effected the psyche of the perpetrators, both male and female. "Rape," states Dorothy Binaifer Nowrojee of the Human Rights Watch, "served to shatter these images by humiliating, degrading, and ultimately destroying the Tutsi woman."[148]

Two months before genocide commenced, gendered propaganda intensified as a structured attempt to influence behaviour categorised Hutu extremist print media. Christopher C. Taylor has noted that in the months preceding genocide violent sexual imagery of both males and females flourished in the iconography of Hutu extremist literature.[149] One picture depicting General Dallaire and Tutsi women which appeared in Kangura in February 1994 presents a clear example of the ways in which Tutsi women were eroticised and sexualised before and during the geno-cide. The cartoon portrays General Romeo Dallaire, Force Commander of UNAMIR, in full uniform with his arms around two Tutsi women.[150] The women are defined by their characteristically stereotypical Tutsi traits: short hair, tall slender frames and European features. Additionally, a caption reading "General Dallaire and his army have fallen into the trap of the Tutsi femmes fatales" also confirmed their ethnicity.[151] Both women are wearing what appears to be UNAMIR uniforms, although their blazers are open, revealing lacy underwear beneath. On the right of Dallaire a woman wearing a badge on her bra which states 'FPR' has her hand on his knee while caressing and kissing the General. On the left, another woman who has a

---

148 Nowrojee et al, Shattered Lives, p. 18.
[149] Taylor, 'A Gendered Genocide,' p. 42.
[150] Kangura No. 56, Rwanda File: Primary Sources from the Rwandan Genocide: R.T.L.M Kangura U.N.S.C. Other, http://www.rwandafile.com/Kangura/k56c1.html [accessed 20/12/11]
[151] Appendix

tattoo on her arm saying 'I love FPR' leans in suggestively towards Dallaire while caressing his other knee. A well-armed soldier stands watch.[152]

The image brings to mind powerful connotations of Tutsis and the UNAMIR peacekeeping mission literally being in bed with one another, as well as evoking impressions of Tutsi women as prostitutes who use their sexual wiles to seduce Western forces stationed in Rwanda.[153] Implications of this image go beyond the message that Tutsi women pose a danger to the safety of Hutus due to their being in league with both the Rwandan Popular Front and the international community. Not only are they not to be trusted politically, but they are also depicted as sexually available to Westerners whilst being unavailable to Hutus. Considering the afore-mentioned precedent of hate media which promoted Tutsi women as superior, this is a dangerous assertion. Spurred on by the belief that Tutsi women were both superior physically and promiscuous sexually, Hutu women were encouraged to envy and despise Tutsi women.

Motivations of female killers undoubtedly had some of their roots in this belief, especially considering the sexual forms of violence which women like Pauline Nyiramasuhuku actively championed. Tutsi women were untrustworthy, promiscu-ous, sexual objects who would gladly jump in bed with the perceived enemy. Tutsi women were stereotyped as arrogant, immoral and hyper sexual deviants.[154] Many Hutu women believed, due to the pervasiveness of these labels, that Tutsi women deserved their fate in the hands of sexual torturers.[155] Effects of propaganda of this nature, of course, cannot be gauged accurately. What is clear, however, is that there was a pervasive media influence which both drew upon traditional concepts of ethnic

---

[152] Appendix
[153] Green, 'Propaganda', pp. 733-776, 733-755.
[154] Blizzard, 'Women's Roles', p. 22.
[155] Ibid.

and gender divides, cementing ideological justification in the minds of Hutu women. In 2003 the International Criminal Tribunal for Rwanda recognised gender propaganda in media and hate speeches as an important component in determining the form of violence against women.[156] Mass rapes were described by the ICTR as a "foreseeable consequence" of propaganda of this nature.[157] Without a precedent of ethnic racism propaganda would have had no foundation, yet, without the reinforcement of these beliefs which media bolstered, and the rationalisation which it provided, sexual crimes against Tutsi women would no doubt have been less prevalent. Gendered propaganda was certainly a powerful tool in motivating women to commit or endorse sexual crimes, yet the strength of hate media and its extensiveness in society were reliant on an already ubiquitous ideology based on ethnic divides which diminished any sense of sisterhood which should perhaps have encouraged Hutu women to feel compassion towards their Tutsi female neighbours.

Gendered propaganda had malicious consequences on perceptions of Tutsis, particularly Tutsi women. Envy and jealousy of Tutsi women took on dangerous form as many Hutu women began to accept these ubiquitous stereotypes. A female inmate in Kigali Central Prison who stood accused of genocide explained that "Hutu women hated and were jealous of Tutsi women. Hutu women were jealous of Tutsis' wealth. Women wanted their goods."[158] In addition to an apparent jealousy based on ethic class divides, Hutu men were also typecast as incapable of resisting the attractions of Tutsi women alone, they needed their Hutu wives, sisters and mothers

---

[156] International Law, 'Genocide. U.N. Tribunal Finds That Mass Media Hate Speech Constitutes Genocide, Incitement to Genocide, and Crimes against Humanity,' Prosecutor v. Nahimana, Barayagwiza, and Ngeze (Media Case), Case no. ICTR-99-52-T (Int'l Crim. Trib. for Rwanda Trial Chamber I Dec. 3, 2003), *Harvard Law Review*, Vol. 117, No. 8 (Jun., 2004), pp. 2769-2776, p. 2775-2776
[157] Ibid.
[158] Female genocide suspect, Kigali Central Prison (interview, respondent #13), 3 July 2001, in Hogg, 'Women's Participation', p. 87.

to call them back to reason. What better way to safeguard those men from the Tutsi seductresses than to eradicate the problem. Once all of the Tutsi women had been removed from society the beauty of the Hutu women could finally shine. There would be no more competition. In a broadcast by Hutu extremist station Radio-Television Libre des Milles Collines, Hutu girls are told: "wash yourselves and put on a good dress to welcome our French allies. The Tutsi girls are all dead, so now you have your chance."[159] Prunier points out that this broadcast, along with other gendered propaganda, provides evidence of a "lingering inferiority complex,"[160] and somewhat accounts for the profound sadism unleashed by Hutus against Tutsi.[161] Envy and resentment are arguably the most social of the emotions, but they are usually experienced in private, scarcely are they discussed or acknowledged to others. When these emotions involve traits like intelligence and physical beauty, it is troublesome to eliminate them. The wealth and power can be won or taken from ones enemies, but intelligence and beauty remain distant goals and cannot be seized from those that one envies.[162]

Hutu women had been just as susceptible to the ideologically motivated othering of Tutsi women as had men, if not more so due to their role as guardian of their ethnicity. A 'them' versus 'us' mentality had governed Rwandan society, arguably since colonialists had emphasised ethnic differences. The potency of expected roles of Hutu women, especially the roles of moral guardian and dedicated member of the Hutu ethnicity, was assigned externally by propaganda, media and the Hutu community itself. These responsibilities were embraced by women who had been denied of other sources of social power. The strength of the ideology should not be underesti-

---

[159] G. Prunier, *The Rwanda Crisis: History of a Genocide* (London: Hurst, 1995) p. 292/ 296.
[160] Prunier, *the Rwanda*, p. 9.
[161] Taylor, 'A Gendered Genocide,' p. 50.
[162] Ibid.

mated. As Lisa Sharlach writes, "in 1994 Rwanda, a woman's loyalty to her ethnic group almost always overrode any sense of sisterhood to women of the other ethnic groups."[163] Sarah Blizzard highlights that in Rwanda there was a precedent of inciting violence based on ethnic identity for material gain.[164] This tactic began with colonisation when first Germany and then Belgium divided the population based on ethnic identities which previously had not existed. All Rwandans share language, religion and cultural identity. In spite of this, the elitist endeavours of the colonists to empower one ethnicity over another led to a disparate society. Tutsis became the superior minority, and this antagonised the majority Hutu population. As a consequence of what Mamdani has described as the construction of political, rather than ethnic identities,[165] there developed a deep ethnic segregation which evolved between Tutsis and Hutus. Although, as earlier discussed, intermarriage was common, there were still those who harboured a preoccupation with defending ethnic purity.[166] A prime catalyst to genocide was a desire for purity in the Hutu ethnic group. This ideological motive is apparent when considering the indiscriminate root and branch killing of Tutsis. Young, old, male, female, none were spared. Evidence also lies in the sexual violence and mutilations which resulted in incapacitating women from reproducing or diluted the Tutsi ethnic gene pool through pregnancy from rape by Hutu men. Ideology is perhaps the most vital component. Without ideological motives genocide would have been unlikely to take shape, none of the other aspects would come together to cause genocide. Ideology, especially the way Hutu women viewed Tutsi women, was created by colonialism and evolved over time to reach a crescendo in the first few months of 1994.

---

[163] Sharlach, 'Gender and Genocide', p. 388.
[164] Blizzard, 'Women's Roles', p. 3.
[165] Mamdani, *When Victims Become Killers*, p. 15.
[166] Blizzard, 'Women's Roles', p. 6.

A multitude of factors drove the genocide, a few components which are per-ceived as the most significant have been mentioned here in detail. Some were more prevalent than others. Some affected women more intensely than men, in particular the gendered propaganda specifically aimed at women of both ethnicities. Each woman had her own personal motives, no one single cause or combination of causes can be cited as the most important. Another factor which many female prisoners have pointed to is sheer opportunism. Greed guided some women to loot the dead and even motivated some to murder. Many women believed the promises of politicians, journalists and local government officials that those who killed would receive rewards, and even inherit the land of Tutsis. Women were encouraged by menfolk and extremists to loot possessions. Looting was a feminine coded task during the genocide which went along with typical gender norms. On the whole though, there was no one set of structural motivations which encouraged women to commit genocide related crimes.

Conclusion

Fundamentally, this genocide could not have spread with the ferocity in which it did were it not for the support, agency, agreement and subsidiary roles played by Rwandan women. Women, thus, far from being solely victims, also must bear some brunt of the moral burden. Women have a doubly difficult challenge to contend with. Their situation is complex, many are both victim and perpetrator, some showed compassion as well as malevolence. Rwandan women's status in society has dramatically changed and their role in society has drastically altered. A shortage of men due to many being dead or imprisoned has left the country in disarray. Women have now taken on roles traditionally reserved for men.[167] To what extent the genocide has contributed to the empowerment of women in the aftermath is an understudied area which merits further consideration.

This dissertation has discovered that female motives for inclusion in the slaughter were not all that dissimilar to males. The most challenging components to dissect are the motives for the sexual violence which was wreaked on Tutsi women. Rape, for the men, served as a warrior's reward, for the women it was clarification that the Tutsis were not as superior as had been widely propositioned. Jealousy, endorsed by gendered propaganda, affected both males and females. Although women and men were jealous of Tutsi females for very different reasons. The men could not have them, and the women could not live up to their reputation as ethnic beauties. Ideology was shared between men and women. Fear and coercion was a shared motive also but the intensity imposed on men and women differed considerably. Men were much more likely to be killed if they did not take part than women. Greed and opportunism was an offshoot of the most potent factors and could not

---

[167] Blizzard, 'Women's Roles', p. 10.

have influenced decisions were it not for the onset of genocide. An intense hatred was triggered in some women due to these circumstances which morphed into a belief that it was their duty to protect their ethnic group. Largely denied authority throughout their lives, many women, stereotyped as ethical core of the family, ironically allowed the small power afforded them during the genocide to override their morality and take to murder.

The purpose of this dissertation was not to present women in an evil light, or to suggest that women have been responsible for the Rwandan genocide to the same level as have men, but to draw attention to the fact that all humans are capable of atrocities, as well as compassion, sometimes bilaterally, whether they be male or female. While this seems like an obvious statement, unfortunately gender conventions mean that women are often stripped of agency. Gender is constructed by social and cultural expectations, if those expectations or performances are altered or diminished by way of a combination of structural forces which were present in Rwanda, motivations such as hate propaganda, jealousy and the other factors discussed herein become more potent, then subsequently women are just as likely to incite, commit or condone violence on a genocidal scale. Women should be recognised as perpetrators instead of solely victims and their actions should not be condoned or diminished by way of searching for excuses which associate moral responsibility with men due to them being the culturally dominant gender.

Where feminist theory is concerned, female perpetrators of the Rwandan genocide present a challenge to feminist schools which assert that women are not violent by nature and even contradict feminist theorists who propose that women are socially programmed to be passive.[168] "We have yet to examine fully the implications

---

[168] Sharlach, 'Gender', pp. 389–390.

for feminist theory of catastrophes such as Rwanda," writes Lisa Sharlach, "in which women are both victims and villains."[169] Most women who held leadership positions in Rwanda, both before and during the genocide, had defied gender expectations to reach this status. Some women had university degrees. Many perpetrators interviewed by Nicole Hogg claimed to have also organised compassionate deeds. Some women hid Tutsis and killed Tutsis. Nyiramasuhuko was supposed to have been interested women's affairs. There is a great difficulty in connecting such beguiling female attributes with brutal acts of mass murder. How can these two conflicting qualities be reconciled? The answer, unfortunately, for many investigators of the genocide and sometimes for Rwandans themselves is to strip these rare women of their femininity altogether and class them as exceptional instances of non-women who betrayed their sex and thus no longer deserve to be classed as women. For example, one Rwandan feminist asserted that Pauline Nyiramasuhuko was "not a woman. She always acted like a man."[170]

Studies involving the roles of women as perpetrators in both the Rwandan genocide and other conflicts remain underdeveloped. Scholars are often concerned with the relationships between victims and perpetrators, the role of the state, the role of the international community, and various motivating factors. However, the dynamics between gender and genocide and how gender expectations guide the progression of genocide development is an area which merits further investigation. A handful of scholars, including Adam Jones, Lisa Sharlach and various feminists have tackled this subject, yet there still remains room for manouvre. Motivations of genocide perpetrators cannot be fully grasped without an understanding of the ways in which socially constructed gender identity has affected the origins of genocide and the

---

[169] Sharlach, 'Gender', p. 388.
[170] Hogg, 'Women's Participation', p. 99.

52

methods of murder which, as in the case of Rwanda, are more often than not gender directed. Genocide is not a stagnant discipline, and for this reason it is important that scholars do not fall into the trap of being subconsciously guided by a societies gendered concept of who should be allocated responsibility as a genocidaire. Women, men, in some cases children, are capable of genocide. Threats on one's status, identity, sense of importance or ethnic survival can have consequences which are difficult to comprehend.

This dissertation has explored the motives and nature of the participation of women in the Rwandan genocide in the context of gender relations in pre-genocide Rwandan society. It has revealed that despite the prominence of a patriarchal Rwandan culture, women were not passive bystanders in the slaughter. Conventional notions of fitting female behaviour nonetheless did regulate and influence women's contribution in the genocide. Many 'ordinary' women were part of the genocide, whether all have been punished or many have escaped justice due to the subsidiary nature of their involvement remains a matter of contention. The nature of women's involvement was at various planes. Though, harmonious with gender traditions, women committed substantially less roles of explicit violence than men. Moral responsibility for women, due to the nature of their roles in comparison to the barbarity of men's actions has been misappropriated in post-genocide Rwanda. This dissertation has left many unanswered questions. There is much scope for future study. Greater consideration as to women's contribution to genocide and the gender relations which must be noted as a significant factor in both the forms which violence took and the roles allowed for women will provide a more comprehensive representation of women's various experiences of mass violence.

Substantiation of argument, whether objectives achieved

Appendices

171

[171] Kangura No. 56, Rwanda File: Primary Sources from the Rwandan Genocide: R.T.L.M Kangura U.N.S.C. Other, http://www.rwandafile.com/Kangura/k56c1.html [accessed 20/12/11]

Bibliography

Primary Sources

Hatzfeld, J., Interviews with perpetrators:

- Hatzfeld, J., A Time for Machetes: The Rwandan Genocide: The Killers Speak: A Report (London: Serpent's Tail, 2005)

Hogg, N., Interviews female with perpetrators:

- Hogg, N., 'Women's Participation in the Rwandan Genocide: Mothers or Monsters', *International Review of the Red Cross,* 92, 877 (2010)

ICTR

- ICTR, Office of the Prosecutor, Butare Cases: Witness Summaries Grid (6 April 2000)

United Nations

- United Nations, *Report on the Situation of Human Rights in Rwanda submitted by Rene Degni-Segui*, Special Rapporteur of the Commission on Human Rights, under paragraph 20 of the resolution S-3/1 of 25 May 1994, E/CN.4/1996/68, January 29, 1996, p. 7

Red Cross

- Hogg, N., 'Women's Participation in the Rwandan Genocide: Mothers or Monsters', *International Review of the Red Cross,* 92, 877 (2010)

Kangura

The Hutu Ten Commandments
- Ngeze, H., 'The Hutu Ten Commandments,' *Kangura*, issue 6 (December 1990)

General Dallaire and the Tutsi femme Fatales
- Kangura No. 56, Rwanda File: Primary Sources from the Rwandan Genocide: R.T.L.M   Kangura   U.N.S.C.   Other, http://www.rwandafile.com/Kangura/k56c1.html [accessed 20/12/11]

RTLM

Broadcast
- Prunier, G., *The Rwanda Crisis: History of a Genocide* (London: Hurst, 1995) p. 292/ 296.

Secondary Sources

1) Adler, R., Loyle, C. and Globerman, J., 'A Calamity in the Neighbourhood: Women's Participation in the Rwandan Genocide', *Genocide Studies and Prevention*, 2, 3 (2007),

2) African Rights, *Rwanda: Death, Despair and Defiance* (African Rights, London, 1995)

3) African Rights, *Rwanda: Not So Innocent: When Women Become Killers* (London: African Rights, 1995)

4) Berry, J. A., & Berry, C. P., eds., Genocide in Rwanda: A Collective Memory (Washington, D.C.: Howard University Press, 1999)

5) Blizzard, S., 'Women's Roles in the 1994 Rwanda Genocide and the Empowerment of Women in the Aftermath,' *Georgia Institute of Technology*, http://smartech.gatech.edu/bitstream/handle/1853/11577/blizzard_sarah_ m_200608_mast.pdf?sequence=1 (2006),

6) Bonneux, L., 'Rwanda: A Case of Demographic Entrapment', Lancet 344, No. 17 (1994), pp. 1689–1690.

7) Burkhalter, H., 'A Preventable Horror? Rwanda', Africa Report, 39, 6 (1994) pp. 17-21.

8) Burkhalter, H., 'The Question of Genocide: The Clinton Administration and Rwanda', World Policy Journal 11, No. 4 (1994), pp. 44–55.

9) Butler, J., *Gender Trouble: Feminism and the Subversion of Identity* (New York: Routledge, 1990)

10)Cook, S. E., Genocide in Cambodia and Rwanda: New Perspectives (London: Transaction Publishers, 2005)

11)Dallaire, Roméo , Shake Hands With the Devil: The Failure of Humanity in Rwanda (London: Arrow, 2005)

12)Des Forges, A., Leave None to Tell the Story: Genocide in Rwanda (New York: Human Right swatch and Fédération Internationale des Ligues des Droits de l'Homme, 1999).

13)Des Forges, A., 'Shame—Rationalizing Western Apathy on Rwanda', Foreign Affairs 79, No. 3 (2000), p. 141.

14)Destexhe, Alain , Rwanda and Genocide in the Twentieth Century (London: Pluto Press, 1995)

15) Drumbl, M. A., 'Punishment, Post genocide: From Guilt to Shame to Civis in Rwanda', in *New York University Law Review*, 75, 5 (2000)

16) Elshtain, J. B., *Thinking about Women and International Violence*, in *Women, Gender, and World Politics: Perspectives, Policies, and Prospects,* edited by P. R. Beckman & F. D.Amico (Westport, CT: Bergin and Garvey, 1994)

17) Emizet, K. N.F., 'The Massacre of Refugees in Congo: A Case of UN Peace-keeping Failure and International Law,' Journal of Modern African Studies 38, No. 2 (2000), pp. 163–202.

18) Erwin, S., Left to Tell: One Woman's Story of Surviving the Rwandan Holocaust by Ilibagiza, Immacule (London: Hay House, 2007)

19) Feil, S. R., Preventing Genocide: How the Early Use of Force Might Have Succeeded in Rwanda (Washington, D.C.: Carnegie Commission on Preventing Deadly Conflict, 1998)

20) Fogelman, E., *Conscience and Courage: Rescuers of Jews during the Holocaust* (New York: Anchor Books, 1994)

21) Friedman, P., *Roads to Extinction: Essays on the Holocaust* (New York: Jewish Pubn Society, 1980)

22) Gendercide Watch, Case Study: Genocide in Rwanda, (1994) http://www.gendercide.org/case_rwanda.html [accessed 10/03/2012]

23) Gourevitch, P. & Kagame, P., 'After genocide', Transition, 72 (1996) pp.162-194.

24) Gourevitch, P., We Wish to Inform You That Tomorrow We Will Be Killed With Our Families: Stories From Rwanda (London: Picador, 1999)

25) Green, L. L., 'Propaganda and Sexual Violence in the Rwandan Genocide: An Argument for Intersectionality in International Law', *Columbia Human Rights Law Review*, 33 (Summer 2002)

26) Gourevitch, P., *We Wish To Inform You That Tomorrow We Will Be Killed With Our Families* (London: Picador, 1999)

27) Gulaid, H., 'Ordinary Women: Understanding Female Agency in Genocide Perpetration,' *Asbarez* (2011) http://asbarez.com/93363/ordinary-women-understanding-female-agency-in-the-perpetration-of-genocide/ [accessed 2/3/2012]

28) Hatzfeld, J., Into the Quick of Life (London: Serpent's Tail, 2005)

29) Hatzfeld, J., A Time for Machetes: The Rwandan Genocide: The Killers Speak: A Report (London: Serpent's Tail, 2005)

30) Heinze, E., 'The Rhetoric of Genocide in U.S. Foreign Policy: Rwanda and Darfur Compared', Political Science Quarterly, 122, 3 (2007) pp. 359-384.

31) Hilsum, L., 'Settling Scores: Ethnic Violence in Rwanda' Africa Report, 39, 3 (2994) pp. 13-17.

32) Hogg, N., 'Women's Participation in the Rwandan Genocide: Mothers or Monsters', International Review of the Red Cross, 92, 877 (2010)

33) Human Rights Watch, Slaughter among Neighbors: The Political Origins of Communal Violence (New Haven, Conn.: Yale University Press, 1995)

34) International Federation of Red Cross and Red Crescent Societies, 'Under the Volcanoes: Special Focus on the Rwandan Refugee Crisis', in World Disasters Report (Amsterdam: Martinus Nijhoff for IFRCRCS, 1994).

35) Itano, N., '3,000 Rwandan Women Await Trials for Genocide' (2002), http://oldsite.womensenews.org/article.cfm/dyn/aid/1152/context/archive [accessed 10/03/2012]

36) Jones, A., 'Gender and Genocide In Rwanda', Journal of Genocide Research, 4, 1 (2002

37) Jones, A., 'Gendercide and Genocide', Journal of Genocide Research, 2, 2 (2010)

38) Jones, A., Gender Inclusive: Essays on Violence, Men, and Feminist International Relations (London: Routledge, 2009)

39) Jones, A., Genocide: A Comprehensive Introduction (London, Routledge, 2010) 2nd Ed.

40) Keane, F., Season of Blood: A Rwandan Journey (London: Penguin Books, 1995)

41) Kiernan, B., Blood and Soil: A World History of Genocide and Extermination from Sparta to Darfur (New Haven, Conn.; London: Yale University Press, 2007)

42) Kuperman, A., 'Rwanda in Retrospect', Foreign Affairs, 79, 1 (2000) pp. 94.

43) Kuperman, A. J., The Limits of Humanitarian Intervention: Genocide in Rwanda (Virginia: Oakland, 2001)

44) Kuperman, A., 'The Other Lesson of Rwanda: Mediators Sometimes Do More Damage than Good', SAIS Review 16, No. 1 (1996), p. 221.

45) Landesman, P., 'A Woman's Work', in NY Times Magazine, 15 September 2002, available at: http://www.nytimes.com/2002/09/15/magazine/a-woman-s-work.html [accessed11/01/2012]

46) Lemarchand, R., The 1994 Rwandan Genocide, in: Totten, S. & Parsons, W. S., Century of Genocide: Critical Essays and Eyewitness Accounts (New York: Routledge, 2009) 3rd Ed.

47) Mamdani, M., 'From Conquest to Consent as the Basis of State Formation: Reflections on Rwanda,' New Left Review No. 216 (1996), pp. 3–36.

48) Mamdani, M., *When Victims Become Killers: Colonialism, Nativism, and the Genocide in Rwanda* (Oxford: James Currey Ltd, 2001)

49) Malkki, L., Purity and Exile: Violence, Memory, and National Cosmology among Hutu Refugees in Tanzania (Chicago: University of Chicago Press, 1995)

50) Magnarella, P. J., Justice in Africa: Rwanda's Genocide, its Courts, and the U.N. Criminal Tribunal (Aldershot: Ashgate, 2000)

51) Meintjes, S., Turshen, M. & Pillay, A.,*The Aftermath: Women in Post-Conflict Transformation* (London: Zed Books, 2001),

52) Melvern, L., A People Betrayed: The Role of the West in Rwanda's Genocide (London: Zed, 2000)

53) Melvern, L., Conspiracy to Murder: The Rwandan Genocide (London: Verso, 2006)

54) Neuffer, E., *The Key to My Neighbours House: Seeking Justice in Bosnia and Rwanda* (London: Picador, 2002)

55) Newbury, C., The Cohesion of Oppression: Clientship and Ethnicity in Rwanda 1860–1960 (NewYork: Columbia University Press, 1988)

56) Newbury, C., 'Rwanda: Recent Debates over Governance and Rural Development,' in Goran B. Hyden, ed., Governance and Politics in Africa (Boulder, Colo.: Lynne Rienner, 1992).

57) Nowrojee, B. & Thomas, D. Q., *Shattered Lives: Sexual Violence During the Rwandan Genocide and its Aftermath* (New York: Human Rights Watch, 1996)

58) Olson, J., "Behind the Recent Tragedy in Rwanda," Geo-Journal 35, No. 2 (1995), pp. 217–222.

59) PBS Frontline Documentary, 'Ghosts of Rwanda' (2004)

60) Patterson, J., 'Rwandan Refugees', Nature No. 373 (1995)

61) Pearson, P., *When She Was Bad: Violent Women and the Myth of* Innocence (New York: Viking, 1997)

62) Percival, V. & Homer-Dixon, T., Environmental Scarcity and Violent Conflict: The Case of Rwanda (Toronto: University of Toronto, 1995)

63) Prunier, G., The Rwanda Crisis: History of a Genocide (London: Hurst, 1998)

64) Rubinstein, W. D., Genocide: A History (Edinburgh: Pearson, 2004)

65) Rwanda: Death, Despair and Defiance (London: African Rights, 1995)

66) Rusesabagina, P. & Zoellner, T., An Ordinary Man (Oxford: Isis, 2008)

67) Schabas, W., 'Hate Speech in Rwanda: The Road to Genocide',

68) McGill Law Journal, 46, 1 (2000) pp. 141-172.

69) Scheper-Hughes, N., 'Small Wars and Invisible Genocides', Social Science and Medicine 43, No. 5 (1996)

70) Sharlach, L., 'Gender and Genocide in Rwanda: Women as Agents and Objects of Genocide', *Journal of Genocide Research,* 1, 3, (1999),

71) Sjoberg L. & Gentry, C. E., *Mothers, Monsters, Whores: Women's Violence in Global Politics* (New York: Palgrave Macmillan, 2007)

72) Smart, C., *Women, Crime, and Criminology: A Feminist Critique* (London: Routledge, 1976)

73) Sperling, C., Mother of Atrocities: Pauline Nyiramasuhuko's Role in the Rwandan Genocide', Fordham Urban Law Journal, 33, 2 (2006) pp. 637-665.

74) Steans, J., *Gender and International Relations: An Introduction* (New Jersey: Rutgers University Press, 1998)

75) Straus, S., 'What is the Relationship Between Hate Radio and Violence? Rethinking Rwanda's Radio Machete', Politics & Society, 35, 4 (2007) pp. 609-638.

76) Straus, S., The Order of Genocide: Race, Power, and War in Rwanda (New York: Cornell University Press, 2008)

77) Taylor, C. C., 'A Gendered Genocide: Tutsi Women and Hutu Extremists in the 1994 Rwanda Genocide,' *PoLAR: Political and Legal Anthropology Review*, 22, 1 (2008) pp. 42-54, p. 42.

78) Taylor, C. C., Sacrifice as Terror: The Rwandan Genocide of 1994 (Oxford, U.K.: Berg, 1999)

79) Thompson, A., *The Media and the Rwanda Genocide* (London: Pluto, 2007)

80) Totten, S. & Parsons, W. S., Century of Genocide: Critical Essays and Eyewitness Accounts (New York: Routledge, 2009) 3rd Ed.

81) Totten, S. & Ubaldo, R., *We Cannot Forget: Interviews with Survivors of the 1994 Genocide in Rwanda* (USA: Rutgers, 2011)

82) Uvin, P., Aiding Violence: The Development Enterprise in Rwanda (West Hartford, Conn.: Kumarian Press, 1998), pp. 67– 68

83) Uvin, P., 'Difficult Choices in the New Post-Conflict Agenda: The International Community in Rwanda after the Genocide', Third World Quarterly 22, No. 2 (2001), pp. 177–189.

84) Uvin, P., 'Prejudice, Crisis, and Genocide in Rwanda,' African Studies Review 40, No. 2 (1997), pp. 91–115; Taylor, Sacrifice as Terror, ch. 2.

85) Uvin, P., 'Reading the Rwandan Genocide', International Studies Review, 3, 3 (2001), pp. 75-99.

86) Waller, J., *Becoming Evil: How Ordinary People Commit Genocide and Mass Killing* (Oxford: Oxford University Press, 2002)

87) Wallis, A., Silent Accomplice: The Untold Story of France's Role in the Rwandan Genocide (London: Tauris, 2007)

88) Watson, P., 'Purging the Evil: Rwanda', Africa Report, 39, 6 (1994) pp. 13

89) Du Preez, W. P., Genocide: The Psychology of Mass Murder (London: Boyars/Bowerdean, 1994)